Four Generations On The Yukon

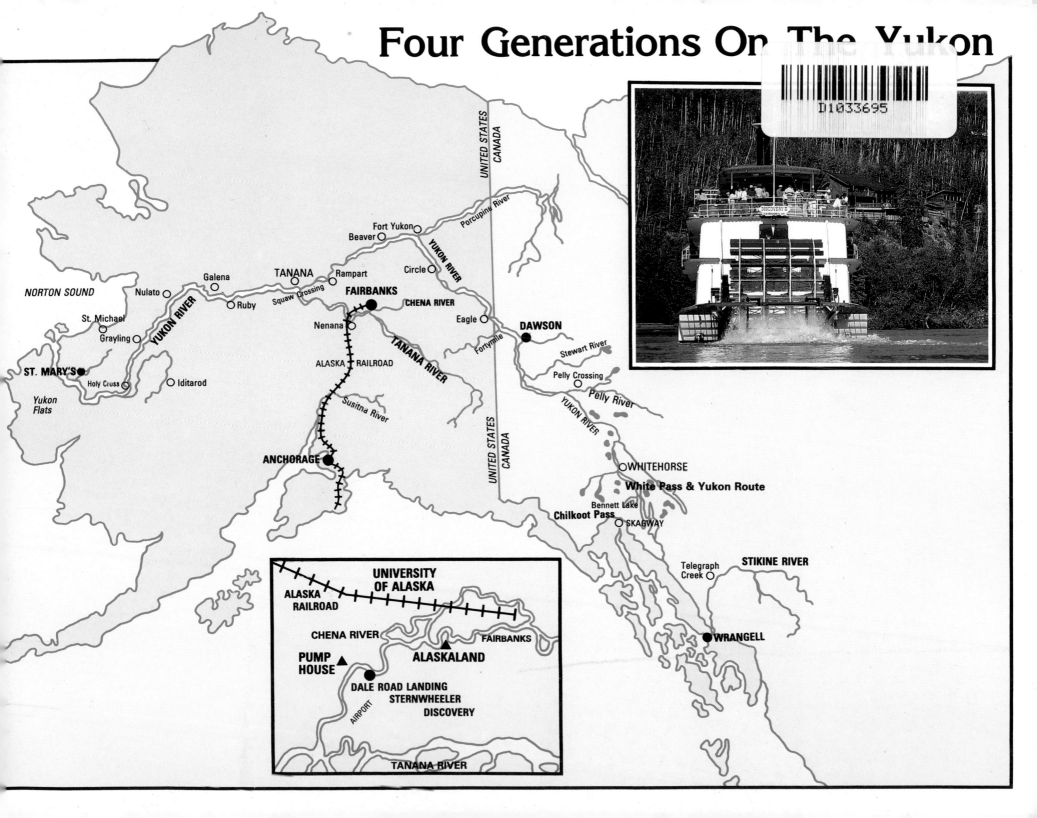

NORTON SOUND

UNITED STATES / CANADA

Fort Yukon
Beaver
Galena
TANANA
Rampart
Circle
Nulato
Ruby
Squaw Crossing
FAIRBANKS
St. Michael
Nenana
CHENA RIVER
Grayling
YUKON RIVER
Eagle
DAWSON
ST. MARY'S
Holy Cross
Iditarod
ALASKA RAILROAD
TANANA RIVER
Fortymile
Stewart River
Yukon Flats
Susitna River
Pelly Crossing
Pelly River
YUKON RIVER
ANCHORAGE

YUKON RIVER

○WHITEHORSE
White Pass & Yukon Route
Bennett Lake
Chilkoot Pass ○ SKAGWAY

Telegraph Creek ○
STIKINE RIVER

●WRANGELL

Inset map
UNIVERSITY OF ALASKA
ALASKA RAILROAD
CHENA RIVER
FAIRBANKS
PUMP HOUSE ▲
▲ **ALASKALAND**
DALE ROAD LANDING
STERNWHEELER DISCOVERY
AIRPORT
TANANA RIVER

Ready for her maiden voyage to Fairbanks, the sternwheeler Discovery III is unloaded at the St. Marys dock on the Andreafsky River, with the Yukon Delta in the background.

On the cover: *Clockwise, from left, Capt. Jim Binkley stands by proudly while the big riverboat is eased onto the tideflats at Freeland, Wash., to await the incoming Puget Sound tide; Nichols Bros. Boat Builders workers paint the wheel of* Discovery III; *at home in Fairbanks, the 156-foot riverboat lands at the Pump House Restaurant to discharge passengers.*

ISBN 0-945397-01-1

Library of Congress
Catalog Card Number 87-83743

Epicenter Press Inc.
P.O. Box 60529, Fairbanks, AK 99706
Printed in Singapore
through Palace Press
of San Francisco

FOUR GENERATIONS ON THE YUKON

Kent Sturgis

Epicenter Press
Fairbanks, Alaska

Table of Contents

Capt. Jim and Mary Binkley, their children, spouses and grandchildren gather on the bow of Discovery III *between cruises.*

Right—*Dog-musher Mary Shields, popular author and veteran long-distance racer, puts on a demonstration for passengers at a stop on the Tanana River near Fairbanks.*

The author, Kent Sturgis, left, joins the crew of Discovery III in this photograph taken near the end of the sternwheeler's maiden voyage up the Yukon River to Fairbanks. Others are, top row, from left, "Buzz" Faulhaber, Skip Binkley, Kent Chappel, Don Dryden, "Rocky" MacDonald, Joe Faulhaber, Bill Farnsworth, Neil McKinnon and Kenny Persinger; on the stairs, from top, Dave Walker and Marc Strachan.

To Albro Gregory, 1911-1987,
a classic newsman who
had hoped to make this voyage.

Preface

The memory is vivid of carefree youngsters hanging on for dear life to a thick hemp rope, swinging from an upper deck of the sternwheeler *Nenana* to the nearby riverbank on a hot, sunny day in Fairbanks. We all were influenced greatly that summer in the late 1950s by a Tarzan movie seen at the Empress Theater.

This 237-foot wooden riverboat, built for the Alaska Railroad in 1933, later was moved to what became the Alaskaland municipal park and was named to the National Register of Historic Places. In 1988, a group of concerned citizens was raising funds to restore the *Nenana*.

The colorful riverboats have been part of the scene in Fairbanks, Alaska, since the city's founding—by steamboat—in 1901.

The sternwheelers are part of contemporary Fairbanks, too, gliding smoothly with a rhythmic churning up and down the Chena River several times each day between May and September. Capt. Jim and Mary Binkley and their four children have operated sternwheel riverboat cruises in Interior Alaska since 1950.

Skip Binkley, a high school classmate, told a gathering of friends in August, 1986, about his family's plans to build a new sternwheeler, the *Discovery III*, and to bring it to Fairbanks by way of the Yukon River the following summer. As a writer and photographer, Skip asked, would I be interested in making the trip? Mentally I leaped out of my chair and let out a Tarzan yell! Count me *in*!

Kent Sturgis

Kent Sturgis

Building
Discovery III

A tarp protects the freshly painted paddlewheel of Discovery III *from spring rains at the Nichols Bros. Boat Builders yard on Whidbey Island, near Seattle.*

The first sight of her on that misty spring day in 1987 took my breath away—as it did again and again in the weeks to come.

Even unfinished, her windows covered and the large red paddlewheel half hidden under a blue tarp in the yard of Nichols Bros. Boat Builders, she attracted attention on Whidbey Island near Seattle.

The *Discovery III* charmed all who came near with her beauty and grace, evoking images of the huge, graceful white paddlewheelers on the Mississippi River and the tough, no-nonsense steamboats that carried hopeful prospectors to the Klondike.

This was no ordinary boat-building project.

The 156-foot, 260-ton sternwheeler was a dream come true for the Binkleys, a pioneer Fairbanks family that had been navigating northern waters for 90 years.

*A 156-foot, 260-ton
sternwheeler takes
shape on Puget Sound*

Her keel laid in October, 1986, the Discovery III
*slowly takes shape during the following winter at the
Nichols Bros. Boat Builders shipyard, where a special
lightweight steel is used to create a riverboat that will
carry 1,000 passengers and float in little more than 3
feet of water.*

The Nichols family has been building boats since 1939, more than 500 of them in half a century. Discovery III was their first, but perhaps not last, sternwheeler. From left are Matthew Nichols, his father Frank and brother Archie.

Matthew J. Nichols, himself a third-generation boat builder, said his family-owned shipyard drew heavily from the Binkley experience in building *Discovery III*.

"There aren't many people in this country who can build a sternwheeler," he said. "We were taught by the Binkleys. Now the Nichols family can carry on this tradition."

Nichols and his brother, Archie, are partners in the shipyard at Freeland, Wash., which employs about 150 workers year-round. Their grandfather, George Nichols, and father, Frank, started building boats on the Columbia River in 1939. They moved north to Washington state in 1963. The family has built more than 500 vessels in 50 years, many of them for Alaskan waters.

Matthew Nichols, president of Nichols Bros., was enthusiastic about the project—the shipyard's first sternwheeler.

"What is more romantic than a sternwheeler with the big paddle rumbling and the steam whistle blowing?" he asked.

The Binkley and the Nichols families got along famously, and still do, in spite of the pressure and stress that naturally come with an eight-month, multimillion dollar effort.

"We never had an argument the whole time we built the boat," Nichols said. "We just talked the same language.

"It was special meeting the Binkley family whose descendants represented boat builders, sternwheelers, and the frontier," he said. "It seemed to parallel where we came from—we were among the first people to build steel boats on the Columbia River. People laughed at my grandfather and father for trying to build steel tugboats and fishing boats. 'It'll never work,' they said, 'it just isn't practical. Wood is the only thing.' "

The two families designed and built more steel and high-technology than wood into the *Discovery III*. Binkley made sure it stood up to the long-standing Alaskan tradition of trust-worthy riverboats that his family has maintained through four generations.

This is the story of the remarkable Binkleys and the maiden voyage of the pride of their sternwheeler fleet. ■

The handsome Discovery III, *right, looms large in the background as shipyard workers pause for a game of basketball during a lunch break.*

To the tide flats the hard way!

There is excitement in Freeland, Wash., as Nichols Bros. shipyard workers walk the 260-ton Discovery III onto the tide flats a few hundred yards away to await the incoming tide which will float the new boat for the first time.

Traffic is detoured inland from a road skirting the little Puget Sound cove as the sternwheeler is tractored slowly across the roadway, left, and down a concrete ramp onto the flats. A small crowd of townspeople gather in the rain with umbrellas unfurled to watch, and other activity in the shipyard comes to a halt. There is a sense of pride and accomplishment in this tight-knit island community where Nichols Bros. is the No. 1 employer.

The Nichols Bros. office, above, takes on the atmosphere of a maternity waiting room as Bill Benjamin, left, Jim Binkley Jr., and Capt. Jim Binkley await with high spirits the floating of the Discovery III.

Jim Binkley Jr. looks on, below, as the big sternwheeler is moved onto the tide flats.

Discovery III *passes the downtown Seattle skyline at dusk after a long day of weight testing monitored by the* *Coast Guard on the Duwamish Waterway. In the tests, many tons of weights are placed unevenly aboard the* *riverboat to prove her stability.*

The First Discovery

**GOLD! GOLD! GOLD! GOLD!
Sixty-eight rich men
on the Steamer Portland
STACKS OF YELLOW METAL!**

The July 17, 1897, headlines in the *Seattle Post-Intelligencer* screamed their confirmation of rumors that had trickled down from the Yukon that winter and spring: A major gold strike had taken place the previous August on what became known as the Klondike River.

Charles M. Binkley, then 17, a hard-working young man with lots of energy, ambition and ideas, found himself in the right place at the right time when he arrived in Seattle that year. Though he had no particular interest in prospecting for gold, he did feel the lure of the Yukon and Alaska. Even Seattle's policemen, firemen and streetcar drivers were quitting their jobs to head for the Klondike.

The next spring, Binkley joined the estimated 30,000 men, some women and a few children who migrated to the new town of Dawson in Yukon Territory in 1897 and 1898.

Binkley's interest was in boats, which were to play a major role in the drama playing itself out

Charlie Binkley, 17, methodically checked off some of the clothing recommended by a Seattle outfitter for his trip north to the Klondike in the spring of 1898.

COMPLETE OUTFIT
FOR ONE MAN FOR ONE YEAR

The following is a list of everything needful for a complete outfit. We again caution you—see to it that you secure everything of the very best quality. We guarantee the quality and correct packing of all outfits sold by us. These prices do not include the price of waterproof sacks for packing. Prices are subject to change without notice.

CLOTHING

1 Slicker Lined Canvas Coat (best), each	$3 00 to $3 50
2 Blanket Lined Overalls (Levi Strauss best), pair	2 50
2 Suits California Flannel Underwear (best grade), suit	4 00
1 Danco—Waterproof and Windproof	2 00
1 pair Wool Gloves	50 to 75
2 suits Mackinaw Underwear, full 24 oz., warranted waterproof and steam shrunk, per suit	3 00
2 Suits Light Weight Underwear, each	$1 00 and 2 00
2 Heavy California Overshirts, each	2 00 and 2 50
2 Cotton Overshirts, each	50 to 1 00
1 Mackinaw Coat, full 36 oz.	4 50
1 pair Mackinaw Pants, full 36 oz., pair	4 00
1 pair Corduroy Pants, pair	$3 00 to 4 00
3 pair Overalls, pair	50
6 pair Heavy Wool Socks, pair	35 to 50
2 pair German Socks, pair	$1 00 to 1 50
6 pair Cotton Socks, pair	25
2 pair California Blankets, pair	$8 00 to 10 00
3 pair Wool Mitts, pair	35 to 75
2 pair Wool Lined Leather Mitts, pair	$1 00 to 1 50
1 Heavy Cap	1 00
1 Wide Brim Hat	$2 00 and 3 00
2 Sweaters, each	$2 00 to 4 00
6 Towels, each	25 to 50
1 pair Heavy Suspenders	35 to 50

SUMMIT OF WHITE PASS MAR. 20-99.

in the Klondike. The prospectors would need transportation and the gold camps would need supplies. On his way to becoming a skilled carpenter, machinist, engine maker and inventor, Binkley earned part of the stake he would need for the trip north making a street marquee for McDougall and Southwick Co., a bustling Alaskan outfitter spread out along First Avenue near the Seattle waterfront.

"We carry in stock everything needed by Alaskan miners and prospectors," the company boasted in its advertisements. McDougall and Southwick offered its recommendations for the "complete outfit for one man, for one year." Binkley, who took an engineer's approach to life's challenges, methodically checked off the clothing and footwear he would need including such practical items as:

—A slicker-lined canvas coat ($3.50);

—Two suits Mackinaw underwear, full 24 oz., warranted waterproof and steam shrunk ($3 each);

—Blanket-lined overalls ($2.50);

—One wide brim hat ($2 or $3);

—Two pair wool-lined leather mitts ($1 to $1.50);

—One pair heavy suspenders (35 to 40 cents);

—One spool of linen thread and a dozen assorted darning needles (15 cents);

—A sleeping bag with pillow and canvas cover ($17.25).

Charlie Binkley hiked into Canada's Yukon Territory with 2,000 pounds of clothing, footwear and provisions en route to the Klondike.

Charlie Binkley felt the lure of the Yukon and Alaska though he did not catch the gold fever that seized nearly 30,000 Klondike stampeders in 1897 and 1898. Charlie was interested in the boats that would play a major role in the gold rush.

Some built rafts to get to the Klondike Gold.

On Lake Bennett, thousands of gold seekers, merchants and con men built home-made rafts and boats to float the last 500-600 miles to the Klondike. Few had riverboating experience.

A series of connected lakes and sections of river, including Miles Canyon, left, lay between the upper Yukon and the Klondike goldfields near Dawson City. Binkley earned $15 to $20 for piloting rafts through the canyon.

Boarding a northbound steamer, Binkley set off for the Klondike. After crossing the torturous Chilkoot Pass near Skagway with a ton of clothing and provisions, he found himself on Lake Bennett. There, thousands of men were building boats and rafts for the 500- to 600-mile trip downriver to Dawson through a series of lakes, canyons and white-water rapids that comprised the upper Yukon River.

Below Lake Bennett, Binkley earned $15 to $20 piloting rafts and as much as $100 guiding boats through the Whitehorse Rapids of Miles

Canyon. He helped bring several steamboats through the canyon with steering oars in the bow and bales of hay tied to the sides to act as bumpers. Many boats were homemade affairs. Some were built in shipyards on the West Coast, disassembled and shipped piece by piece to the upper lakes for reassembly. One of those was the *A.J. Goddard*, a 15-ton steamboat whose hull was built in San Francisco. She was the first boat from the upper Yukon to arrive at Dawson, tying up there on June 21, 1898.

Charlie Binkley was well-suited for work on the Yukon. Although he came from a farming family whose ancestors had migrated to America from Switzerland in the 1700s, Binkley had ties to the Mississippi and Missouri rivers, where his father rafted logs to supplement his farm income. A native of Fort Wayne, Indiana, Binkley rafted with his father, found work in boatyards, and was learning to pilot on the Ohio River when a national depression and a case of wanderlust prompted him to head west.

The first season after his arrival in the north, Binkley joined the crew of the 193-ton sternwheeler *Bailey*, built on Lake Bennett.

After some seasoning, Charlie Binkley and his partner, Sid Barrington, built a steamboat at Whitehorse and formed their own transportation company. Sometime between 1908 and 1910, the pair are believed to have built the first of a series of riverboats, the *Hazel B*, in Dawson.

Competition was fierce on the Yukon River. Before the end of the 1898 season, a total of 32 companies operated 60 steamboats, eight tugs and towboats and 20 barges on or near the river.

The Binkley-Barrington strategy was to serve the narrower, shallower and swifter side streams that the larger companies ignored. The partners carried equipment and supplies to miners on such Yukon tributaries as the White River, the Pelly, the Stewart, the Fortymile and the Porcupine.

"Whenever there was a strike, they'd be right on top of it," said Charlie Binkley's son, Jim. "And they'd be paid off in gold dust right on the spot."

It is not known exactly how many vessels the partners built and operated in the Yukon drainage but *Pacific Motor Boat* magazine reported Barrington had ordered twin 48-horsepower motors as late as 1913 for a "freighting scow" built by Charlie Binkley, "who is now making quite a specialty of shallow-draft river boat work."

A native of Fort Wayne, Indiana, Charlie Binkley worked on the Mississippi, Missouri and Ohio rivers before heading west.

The Dawson, *a 779-ton sternwheeler built in Whitehorse, Y.T., in 1901 for the British-Yukon Navigation Co., was wrecked in Rink Rapids in 1926. Charlie Binkley helped guide boats through upper Yukon white water during the Klondike gold rush.*

Charles M. Binkley, 1880-1925

to reach Dawson in the spring and the last to leave there in the fall."

"Sid was flamboyant—a gambler, a mover," said Jim Binkley. "My dad was too busy building boats and operating the machinery to be out there in the front with a big cigar in his mouth. They were the perfect match."

Indeed, if Barrington was a promoter, Binkley was a fixer. Binkley could repair virtually anything, anytime, anywhere—a valuable skill on the Yukon River where the season was short (early June to mid-October) and boatyards were few.

"Binkley will build the boat in Seattle and it will then be knocked down and shipped to Alaska, as it is necessary to haul the frames in over 80 miles of ice from Whitehorse to the point where the boat will be used on the White River," the magazine reported. "She will be reassembled by Binkley in the North and will be used for carrying passengers and freight into the Shushana mining district." The area also was known as the "Chisana" district.

In 1937, writer Clarence Andrews described Barrington as "the daredevil of the Yukon, who is said to never have drifted a bend with his steamboat in his career, who was always the first

The first season after his arrival in the north, Charlie Binkley joined the crew of the 193-ton sternwheeler Bailey, *built on Lake Bennett.*

23

A protected anchorage on Ship Creek became headquarters for construction of the new federal railroad. The camp's population lived mostly in tents, grew to 2,000 by 1915 and became known as Anchorage.

In 1914, as gold production declined in the Klondike, Barrington and Binkley found a new challenge: running freight boats on the Susitna River to support construction of the Alaska Railroad. That year, Congress authorized building of a railroad linking the Gulf of Alaska with the river shipping routes of Alaska's great Interior.

A protected anchorage at the mouth of Ship Creek in Southcentral Alaska was chosen as the construction camp and headquarters for the Alaska Engineering Commission. The camp's population, residing mostly in tents, had grown

In 1914-15, Charlie Binkley and his partner, Sid Barrington, helped move freight up the Susitna River for construction of the Alaska Railroad. In all, they built four shallow-draft riverboats for the Susitna.

to 2,000 by 1915 and Anchorage was on its way to becoming Alaska's largest city.

President Woodrow Wilson selected the Susitna River route for the new railroad in April, 1915. Charles Binkley and Sid Barrington built four shallow-draft riverboats (called the B&B 1, 2, 3 and 4) to carry railroad surveyors, construction crews and supplies up the silty river from its mouth on Cook Inlet.

When the government took over operation of their Susitna boats, Binkley and Barrington looked for another river to run. In 1916, the partners built the 88-foot, 100-horsepower, twin-screw *Hazel B No. 2* on Ship Creek. They loaded her aboard a barge and headed for the Stikine River near Wrangell, in Southeast Alaska.

The rapid 1,000-foot fall of the Stikine from its headwaters in the coastal mountains of Canada to salt water in just over 150 miles offered a navigational nightmare. But where there was a need, there was a way. Three gold rushes had brought prospectors, traders and riverboat men to the Stikine beginning in 1861. The southernmost coastal route into the Klondike, and one of the most difficult, the Stikine River led prospectors to the mountains beyond

Designed and built by Charlie Binkley, the 65-foot, 100-horsepower Hazel B. No. 4 *was launched at Wrangell in 1919 for service on the Stikine River.*

which were the headwaters of the Yukon River.

The Stikine was never the same after Binkley and Barrington arrived.

Until then, steamboats operated by Hudson's Bay Co. and other large trading companies had dominated the river. The old wood-burning boats were slow and required a large crew.

"The river steamer *Nahlin* arrived down from her trip to Telegraph Creek last Thursday morning. The *Nahlin* made the trip to Telegraph Creek and back in about six days' running time, although they were forced to wait at the canyon for several days on account of high water," the *Wrangell Sentinel* reported on July 15, 1916.

The next year, Binkley designed and built the *Hazel B No. 3*, another in the series of boats named after Barrington's wife. The new boat was fast, and could be operated by as few as three men.

"NEW RIVERBOAT BREAKS ALL RECORDS," the *Sentinel* reported on Aug. 2, 1917.

"The new boat left Thursday night on her maiden trip, breaking all previous records for navigation up the Stikine. The voyage from Wrangell to Telegraph Creek, a distance of 152 miles, was made in 26 hours, the fastest time by long odds that was ever made by any boat on the Stikine," the newspaper reported.

"The captain informs us the boat will easily make the trip in 24 hours. This quick time is all the more appreciated when one considers that the Stikine is a swift mountain stream with numerous riffles, and from the mouth of the river to Telegraph Creek is almost a constant climb. But these obstacles are nothing to the new boat which skims along lightly and at places seems almost to jump forward up the stream like a salmon on its way to a fresh-water spawning ground."

The 62-foot riverboat, which weighed less than 10 tons, was propelled by a 95-horsepower, 6-cylinder engine.

"The boat is a genuine Alaskan product," the *Sentinel* reported enthusiastically. "It was designed and built by Capt. Charles Binkley, an Alaskan, and the timber used in its construction is from the Willson and Sylvester Mill at Wrangell. The planking is of fir, while the house is constructed of native spruce and cedar.

"The success of the *Hazel B III* is not an accident. Capt. Charles Binkley, the designer and builder, is a skilled carpenter and cabinet-maker and also a man whose experience navigating northern streams gives him the most intimate knowledge of the requirements."

In June, 1919, Binkley designed and built the twin-screw *Hazel B No. 4* and the *Wrangell Sentinel* reported Binkley had revolutionized the design of riverboats.

"The new boat possesses the quality of springiness, being constructed so that the bottom will bend up and down with the stream to a certain extent, thereby giving a tremendous advantage over boats possessing more rigidity," the newspaper reported.

Part of what made Binkley's Stikine boats unique was an improvement on the tunnel design for the propeller shafts. Fitted with a ball joint, the aft portion of the shafts could be lifted high in the tunnel using a hand-crank in the wheelhouse. This allowed the riverboat to navigate in water as shallow as 18 inches. In deeper water, the propeller shaft was lowered to its normal operating position for maximum speed and efficiency.

The partners carried miners, traders, trappers, hunters, freight, mail, and even a few tourists.

A *Sentinel* reporter told of a pleasure trip aboard the handsome riverboat:

"The scenic beauties of the trip left nothing to be desired. The parties spent all their waking hours from four or five in the morning to near midnight on the deck so as to enjoy everything to the utmost. They were burned and tanned and lost hours of sleep but they missed nothing, including three substantial meals each day."

A series of Stikine riverboats all were named the Hazel B *after the wife of Charlie Binkley's partner, Sid Barrington.*

Designing, building speed boats was Charlie's passion

Charlie Binkley gave an advertising testimonial for propellers made by the Anchor Boat Co. in Seattle after his racing boat, the Seattle Spirit, *won its class in the Pacific Coast Championship. Top speed: 32.4 miles per hour.*

Boats were Charles Binkley's private passion as well. He often wintered in Seattle, living on Lake Union and elsewhere near Puget Sound, where he built racing boats.

With his half-brother, Emerson Reid, Charlie Binkley put together syndicates of investors to finance his expensive hobby. The two men had built the *Seattle Spirit* for competition in the 1909-10 Yukon-Pacific Exposition in Seattle. This slick, 32-foot racing boat was equipped with a 100-horsepower, 6-cylinder Scripps engine.

Seattle Spirit won the Pacific Coast championship in the 10-meter class in 1910, defeating a racing boat called the *Pacer II.*

"At the crack of the gun, they both leaped across the line at a 20-mile clip," *Pacific Motor Boat* magazine reported. "As they sped off down the course, they were so close together no one could see which was in the lead. A great deal of interest was attached to this race, and everyone was yelling and throwing their hats in the air. They ran the first half of the course nearly side by side. Being able to make a shorter turn, *Seattle Spirit* led her rival by over a hundred yards on the home stretch."

The same year, the speedboat made a 30-mile run at an average speed of 32.4 miles per hour and was "conceded to be the fastest boat on the Pacific Coast," the magazine reported.

The racing team of Charlie Binkley and Emerson Reid, Binkley's half-brother, and their speed boat the Wigwam *were featured on the July, 1912, cover of* Pacific Motor Boat.

Binkley is believed to have raced in Canada, Washington, Oregon and California and there is evidence he also designed high-speed power-boats for use on the Great Lakes and Mississippi River as well.

In one memorable race, Binkley and Reid's boat began to take on water after a piece of debris on the course tore out the transom. They won, sinking as they crossed the finish line, and the two men went overboard. Binkley tied his life jacket to the bow line, then made for shore. Undaunted, they dispatched a diver to the spot, pulled the damaged racing boat onto a barge, made repairs, and raced the next day!

Charles Madison "Jim" Binkley Jr. was about a year old when his picture was taken with his father in 1921. Jim was 5 when pneumonia took his father's life.

On one of his trips south, Charlie Binkley met Fannetta "Peggy" Ordway in San Francisco, married her and brought her back to Wrangell. She was a passenger aboard the *Hazel B No. 4* on her maiden voyage in June, 1919.

Charles Madison "Jim" Binkley Jr. was born at Wrangell on May 16, 1920.

Sadly, just as his own father had died at a young age, Charlie Binkley was claimed by pneumonia at age 45 in Seattle in 1925. Jim was 5. Attending high school in northern California, Jim had to wait for his chance to get onto the river, and went north immediately after graduation.

In 1940, Jim's mother, a vivacious woman of Irish descent, met Vincent E. "Vince" James at Shamrock Creek, a mining claim near Fairbanks. They were married soon after.

Three years later, the couple moved to Eagle where they bought and operated the Steel Roadhouse near Fort Egbert on the banks of the Yukon River. They also operated a wood camp near the Alaska-Canada border, supplying wood for the sternwheelers.

Vince and Peggy James moved back to Fairbanks in 1946 and for the next dozen years Vince was superintendent of buildings and grounds at the University of Alaska while Peggy, a nurse, helped care for Dr. Charles E. Bunnell, founding president of the university, in his final years. The Jameses' moved to Portland, Ore., in the late 1950s because of Peggy's poor health. She died in Portland in 1972.

Meanwhile, young Jim Binkley had become a river pilot just in time to see the end of the steamboat era, and to work on the last of the proud sternwheelers.

At age 17, Jim Binkley was a Sea Scout in northern California, where he graduated from high school before heading north to attend the University of Alaska at Fairbanks.

Binkley crewed a season with his father's old partner, Sid Barrington, in Wrangell in 1939, then made his way to Fairbanks in 1940 where he immediately went to work as a deckhand aboard the *Idler*, a 62-foot sternwheeler built in

Charlie Binkley met his future wife, Fannetta "Peggy" Ordway, on a trip to San Francisco. A nurse, Peggy Binkley remained in Alaska after her husband's death in 1925 and eventually remarried.

Fairbanks about 1910 by the Noyes family. After lying in Noyes Slough for many years, the vessel was bought by independent riverboat operator George Black, who converted it from a steamboat to a diesel with a chain-driven sternwheel. It was aboard the *Idler* that Jim Binkley acquired his first sternwheeler experience as Black carried freight and passengers on the Yukon River and its tributaries.

F.G. NOYES STEAM YACHT IDLER.

Jim Binkley acquired his first sternwheeler experience as a deckhand and later as a pilot aboard the 62-foot riverboat Idler *built by the Noyes family in Fairbanks about 1910.*

Last of the Sternwheeler Era

Binkley recalled this time as "the marvelous days in faith and trust of early Alaska."

"I think of those colorful times when the steamboats burned wood, of the times when the woodcutter was not at his woodpile when we came by," Binkley said. "He would leave his name in a Mason jar and the amount of wood he cut, and when he cut it, and how dry it was. The purser would take note of how much wood was taken and he'd peel off the currency and stick it in the jar and put the lid back on. When the fellow came by, he could pick up his money."

While attending the University of Alaska in Fairbanks on a small hill overlooking the Tanana Valley, off and on before and after World War II, Binkley served on a small fleet of riverboats, as a deckhand, and in the engine room, galley and wheelhouse. In addition to the *Idler*, George Black operated the smaller *Kusko* and *Pelican* and the tiny *Mudhen*, all moving cargo, mail and a few passengers. The passengers included miners, government people, school teachers, hunters, and families of Indians setting up summer fish camps to catch the migrating Yukon salmon.

It was on the Yukon and Tanana rivers that Binkley came to admire the Athabascan Indians of Interior Alaska. In most villages, the people still came to the riverbank with a formal greeting as the first riverboat of the season arrived. Clad in mooseskin jackets and intricate and colorful beadwork—their traditional clothing made from animals they hunted to survive—the native people sang and danced at what in the early 1940s was an important occasion.

This was before airplanes brought in the heavy mail. Steamboats carried the mail during the summer; dog teams moved it in winter.

Binkley said the villages were independent and self-reliant in those days. "The trading post was in the middle of town," he said. "The families were close and there was a great deal of love. Everyone had a friendly, outgoing attitude."

He is saddened by the decline of traditions among the native people, but he marvels at the strength and survival skills of these people who anthropologists believe migrated to the Western Hemisphere over a land bridge that crossed what is now the Bering Strait.

"They're amazing people," Binkley said. "Just think of living in this country before contact with western culture. If you and I were Indians living here at that time, we would be responsible for the very survival of our families. What we would eat tomorrow would depend on what we would get today. By taking animals, outwitting them, killing them with primitive weapons, teamwork among the whole family, surviving in a hostile environment through cunning, shrewdness and determination.

"Imagine going out and getting that moose or bear with a spear made of a sharpened shin bone lashed with rawhide to the end of a pole," Binkley said, "and a weapon made out of a stone, a piece of rock lashed to the end of a club.

"And he had to be patient, sitting there for hours, waiting for those animals, outsmarting them, then physically killing them, cutting them up with a sharp rock and getting the skin off so his mate could tan it and make clothes. And he'd get the meat and use the bones for tools and weapons, truly a remarkable people."

Later, to supplement their subsistence hunting, the Athabascans earned cash by trapping, fishing and cutting wood for the steamboats, and working as deckhands and pilots.

Gradually, a number of Athabascans learned the river trade and owned boats of their own. And Binkley, too, moved up.

Binkley loved the challenge and excitement of running the rivers, especially when he worked his way onto the top deck and into the wheelhouse.

As a pilot, Binkley trained himself to be alert, watching the natural forces that affect the shallow-draft riverboats: the shifting channel, riffles on the water, movement of slicks on the surface, the sandbars, and "the biggest enemy of a riverboat operator"—the wind.

"It's like flying an airplane," said Binkley, who later learned to fly one. "Hours can go by with nothing happening, then suddenly everything is happening at once."

Pilots must learn the river four ways: upstream, downstream, daylight and dark. Going with the current can be an exciting ride.

"Coming downstream, you're going fast," Binkley said. "You have that tremendous weight. It's like driving a big truck down an icy hill.

Binkley worked on the Kusko *and other riverboats operated by George Black prior to World War II, recalling this time as "the marvelous days of faith and trust in Alaska."*

You're not steering, you're sliding. You judge the slide. The bigger the boat, the more weight you have, the more critical the judgment is.

"The river is more forgiving going upriver than down because the current, acting as a brake, can slow you down quickly."

Binkley says an experienced pilot relies heavily on instinct, and he swears some veterans can "feel" through their feet the depth of the water beneath the boat.

The natural elements are not always predictable. The season is barely four months long and sometimes the riverboats and their barges became frozen in while heading for their home ports in the late fall.

In 1942, heading up the Tanana River to Nenana, a number of boats and barges were trapped by a sudden, hard freeze.

"The ice started running real heavy," Binkley recalled. "The side streams were making the ice. It was coming into the main channel with a 'shssss-shssss' sound. It was gathering up like acres of ground in front of us.

Attending the university in winter, working the rivers in summer, Jim Binkley served his apprenticeship aboard the Kusko.

"We saw we were going to get stuck, so the idea then was to get off the main river because in the spring those ice cakes can be devastating."

The crews pulled the boats into a nearby tributary and winterized them, then flew out in a bush plane that landed on a snowy sandbar.

The following spring, a crew was flown back in to get the boats ready for a new season.

Binkley was assigned to walk 40 miles downriver to care for a barge frozen in at Squaw Crossing, near the confluence of the Tanana and Yukon, as well as a tugboat at the village of Tanana on the far side of the Yukon. Binkley thought he might make it in a day or two. With the river ice melting behind and in front of him, the hike took nearly a week and Binkley was bone weary and cold by the time he reached a trapper's cabin at the crossing. Finishing his work there, young Binkley stuffed into his pockets biscuits and bacon kindly furnished by the trapper's wife and set out for the big river, a few miles away. His ordeal was not over.

"I finally got to the banks of the Yukon and as far as I could see either way was water," Binkley recalled. "Water from the Tanana and other streams had covered the ice. I cut myself a long pole and felt around—there was ice under the water. I thought I could walk across. So I went across the river, probing for holes.

"Got right up to about here," Binkley said, pointing high on his chest. "Then a little chopping wind started coming up."

Binkley pauses in telling the story, shaking his head in wonder that he made it to Tanana. But he did, wading across the ice-water overflow nearly up to his neck, arriving in the village wet and half-frozen.

World War II On The River

In 1944, Binkley earned his first command, serving two years as master of an Army boat carrying freight on the Yukon. It had been built in 1932 in Seattle for Sid Barrington and his brother, Hill.

The war temporarily slowed the decline of river traffic. Japan had attacked U.S. bases in the Aleutian Chain, and for strategic reasons the military wanted to open more than one supply route into Alaska and the Yukon.

On the Stikine, the Barringtons carried construction materials and equipment into northern British Columbia to build airfields. Meanwhile, the White Pass and Yukon Route, a narrow-guage railroad built after the Klondike strike, moved freight from Skagway to Whitehorse, Y.T., where it was loaded onto riverboats for delivery to construction sites for roads and airfields for the Lend-Lease program that helped resupply the Russians, then an ally in Europe. Much of the freight and fuel came over the Alaska Railroad at Nenana, a busy port on the Tanana River near Fairbanks, where it was transferred to a fleet of civilian and military vessels.

Jim Binkley worked both as a civilian pilot aboard military vessels, and as a pilot and captain for the Army Transportation Corps, working on the rivers during the summer and in the Gulf of Alaska and along the Aleutian Chain in winter.

At times during the war, Binkley recalled, the Army operated more boats in Alaska—landing craft, troop ships, riverboats, barges and tugs—than the Navy and Coast Guard combined.

Running freight along the coast out of Whittier, Cordova and Seward was hard work and many crew members were Alaskans who acquired a reputation for sailing into adverse weather, Binkley said.

"The military amenities were not observed," he said. "When we tied alongside a Navy boat, or a Coast Guard boat, the officers were appalled because we'd come storming across their decks to come ashore. And we might have on a pair of Navy dungarees, and an Army jacket and Air Force boots—whatever came along. We were stepchildren in many respects, so we foraged for ourselves. We didn't look like a military crew!"

Binkley also served on several large sternwheelers during the war, and kept a notebook in which he carefully recorded statistics and other information about the boats he saw and worked aboard. The knowledge was to come in handy.

For a time, Binkley was a pilot aboard the *Aksala*, a 642-ton sternwheeler built at Whitehorse in 1913 by the Alaska Yukon Navigation Co. During the war, it was leased by Sid Barrington from the British Yukon Navigation Co. As an Army pilot, Binkley also was assigned to a trip aboard the *Klondike II*, another BYN sternwheeler built in Whitehorse. Among other things, this handsome riverboat pushed barge-loads of equipment to be used at Ladd Field, later to become Fort Wainwright, near Fairbanks.

Some of the sternwheeler captains and pilots called out of retirement during the war had known and worked with Charlie Binkley. One

of these men with a lifetime of experience on the Yukon was Capt. Charlie Coghlin, who kept a close eye on his pilots while they did most of the steering.

Binkley recalls a memorable landing before an appreciative riverbank audience in Circle City aboard the *Klondike II*. The pilot, Guy Street, made a tricky S-curve around two sandbars, then nudged one of her barges onto a bar, letting the current carry the sternwheel slowly around.

Street completed the skillful maneuver by putting the sternwheel hard in reverse, pulling the barge off the bar and backing into the channel—completely turned around.

"And old Charlie Coghlin is sitting beside me, smoking his pipe, watching all this," Binkley remembers. "And he gets up. Now we're headed straight for shore and getting ready to land. So he steps up, pushes Guy Street to one side, and says 'OK, Street, I'll take over now.'

During World War II, Jim Binkley served aboard the Barry K, *an olive-drab boat operated by the Army. The* Barry K *moved freight and fuel to Galena for the lend-lease airfield used to refuel U.S.-built aircraft headed for the Soviet Union.*

"And we'd come all the way from Dawson and he hadn't touched the wheel. Street shook his head and smiled. And the captain landed the boat and waved his hat and everybody assumed he'd made that remarkable maneuver!

"Charlie Coghlin had been a great pilot in his day and we all agreed he deserved any glory afforded him."

After the war, Binkley was laid up for months when his lungs were frostbitten mushing a borrowed dog team from Eagle village to visit his mother and stepfather at their woodcamp 20 miles away. The temperature had plunged to 48 below zero at the isolated camp on the Yukon near the Canadian border.

Binkley's lips had turned blue and he couldn't breathe. His mother may have saved her son's life by giving him Adrenalin injections from her emergency medical-supply kit until a landing strip could be stamped out in the snow, and a ski-equipped mail plane evacuated him to Fairbanks.

After his recuperation, Binkley returned to the University of Alaska, where he met and fell in love with Mary Hall, a student from Oregon, in the spring of 1946. He was 26; she had just turned 20. Jim was going to school while working part-time at the UA power plant, and running the river during the summer. Mary, a warm and energetic woman, was holding down three different part-time jobs in between classes.

Mary Hall was born in 1926 in Vernonia, Ore., a sawmill and logging town near Portland. Her three brothers caught and processed fish commercially and she still has relatives in Kodiak, a major island fishing port in the Gulf of Alaska.

Persuaded to come to the University of Alaska by a cousin who was a music professor there, Mary was one of 13 incoming freshmen at the small land-grant college in the fall of 1944. By

Capt. Jim and Mary Binkley bought the Godspeed, *a 50-foot, gas-powered propeller boat, from the Episcopal Church and went into the river cruise business in 1950.*

today's standards, it was a long, grueling trip north. Mary boarded a Canadian Pacific plane in Vancouver, B.C., spent a night in Prince Rupert because of bad weather, then overnighted again in Whitehorse before catching the Pan American World Airways flight to Fairbanks.

It was raining when the plane landed in Weeks Field on Aug. 24, 1944, and the taxi nearly got stuck in the mud on Cushman Street in mid-town Fairbanks en route to the university. Few streets were paved.

Mary and Jim were married in Portland in 1946. Their oldest son, Charles Madison "Skip" Binkley III was born in 1948. James "Jim" Binkley Jr. followed in 1950, John Emerson (Johne) Binkley in 1953 and Marilee Ann

West, one of the first to recognize the potential of tourism in the future state, had leased airplanes from Wien to move tour groups around Alaska. But there wasn't enough to do in Fairbanks to keep the tourists entertained.

West found out that Jim Binkley had a river pilot's license and he approached Jim and Mary at the university with a proposition: If the Binkleys would offer a riverboat cruise, West would supply the passengers. The Episcopal Church was selling the *Godspeed*, a 50-foot, gasoline-powered missionary boat because its new bishop, William Gordon, was an airplane pilot and preferred flying to floating. The propeller-driven *Godspeed* could carry 25 passengers.

The deal was made. With a $4,000 loan from the Alaska National Bank, the Binkleys went into the riverboat cruise business while Jim worked full-time and built a home on the side. Mary organized the business side of things in their home and was the operation's "office staff" for years. The business was a success from the start.

Like his father, Jim Binkley was a builder and a fixer and under his hand, the *Godspeed* was undergoing changes constantly. For every hour spent carrying passengers, the *Godspeed* and the riverboats that followed underwent hours of maintenance and repair. The boats had to be winterized in the fall, and made ready in the spring. That, Binkley said, is the hidden side of riverboating.

"People get the idea about how romantic it is, and marvelous, and it's all ice cream and cookies. It's back-breaking work."

And Binkley loved it.

Capt. Jim and Mary Binkley and their sons Skip and Jim posed for a Christmas card photo taken aboard the Godspeed *after their second season.*

Binkley in 1958. All four children were born in Fairbanks. For a time, Jim handled all the maintenance at St. Joseph's Hospital, helped run the UA power plant and built a few houses on the side to support his family.

Opportunity knocked on the young couple's door in 1950.

Chuck West was a pilot who had flown over the Hump in China during the war and later worked as a pilot for Wien Air Lines. He founded Westours and developed it into one of Alaska's largest and most successful tour companies.

In the early 1950s, Jim Binkley loaded his passengers on the Tanana River because the Fairbanks Exploration Co. (FE Co.) was pumping so much muck into the Chena River from its gold-mining operation in Ester that the river became unnavigable. The company's permit from the Corps of Engineers required it to maintain a 3-foot channel but because Binkley was operating the only riverboat on the river at that time, the big mining company decided it was less expensive to lease a bus for Binkley and pay him to transport his passengers to the Tanana. (The Chena Pump House, where the silty overburden from the hydraulic mining was emptied into the Chena, today is a popular Fairbanks restaurant listed on the National Register of Historic Places.)

Binkley was a one-man show at first.

"I'd drive the bus down with maybe 15 people," he recalled. "I'd tell 'em to wait for the boat that will be appearing in a few minutes. Then I'd run down through the trees. I'd jump on the boat and fire it up, get the chairs out, put on my captain's hat, kick it in gear, shove it against the bank, and put the gangway down."

"Hello, I'm the captain," he announced to the surprised tourists. Often he'd find a volunteer to serve the coffee and doughnuts packed by Mary.

Mary Binkley played a significant role from the start. She was on board much of the time and it was her natural outgoing friendliness that helped shape the successful format of the Binkleys' operation today. The children were brought aboard at an early age and given chores and responsibilities as soon as they could handle them.

"We weren't afraid to do hard work," Mary recalled. "Jim was a good 'PR' person, and did the mechanical part and the dreaming, and I did a lot of the background work and made suggestions on the commentary because I felt that's what people wanted—to find out about the native people particularly."

Mary Binkley became a regular member of the crew in the summer of 1951, even though Jim Jr. was due to be born in July. "In mid-June when we started, I looked like I'd swallowed a watermelon, so I just helped once or twice that year," Mary said. "One old fellow from Boston said to Jim, as I was taking down aluminum folding chairs, 'do you think your daughter should be doing that?' That was the last time Jim let me go that summer!"

The Binkleys' old friend and Yukon River pilot, Pete Simple, an Athabascan from Fort Yukon,

The Godspeed's *last year was 1955, when Jim Binkley and Bill English built the first* Discovery *sternwheeler.*

Pete Simple of Fort Yukon, Capt. Jim Binkley's first crewman, joined the Godspeed *in 1952 and for a half-dozen years explained the Athabascan culture to the Binkleys' passengers.*

In 1955, Mary and Jim Binkley christened the Discovery, *with Jim Jr. looking on from the* Godspeed.

came aboard as a deckhand and all-round mate. It was about then Binkley and Simple started dreaming about building a small sternwheeler.

Those were the years when 10 or 15 passengers was a good load, and the relationship between the Binkleys and their passengers was close.

In 1955, the Binkleys went into partnership with Bill English, a Wien flyer who later became director of operations for MarkAir, and Jim Binkley built his first sternwheeler, the *Discovery,* from the ground up in his back yard on Noyes Slough. Capacity: 49 passengers.

Two years later, Binkley and English bought the *Pelican*, a 62-foot diesel propeller boat from the estate of George Black, and until Alaska statehood in 1959 operated an independent passenger and freight service on the Yukon River.

One spring, Binkley built a 60,000-gallon tanker barge and a tug, the *Skookum*. Like most of his building projects, the barge took shape quickly. "We got it into the water in 32 days," he said.

Binkley couldn't sit still as far as his sternwheeler was concerned. By 1959, he had lengthened the *Discovery* twice, once literally cutting the boat in two pieces, pulling them apart with a tractor, and building a new section of hull and superstructure in the gap. Capacity: 150 passengers. His father once had stretched a boat the same way in Dawson.

Mary Binkley was supportive through all these projects in the back yard, although her enthusiasm may have been stretched a little thin when Jim decided the twin smokestacks he had built onto *Discovery* were not historically correct and he set out to replace them with a single stack. The couple worked hard. Mary was running the office, selling tickets and doing much of the behind-the-scenes work, not to mention taking care of the children, running the household and taking part in a variety of community and school activities.

Capt. Jim couldn't keep his hands off first 'Discovery'

Discovery, the first sternwheeler, was christened in 1955 and Capt. Jim Binkley made improvements every winter. By 1959, he had lengthened Discovery twice, once literally cutting the boat in two pieces, pulling them apart with a tractor, and building a new section of hull and superstructure in the gap.

Five lives of Discovery I

Following off-season "remodeling" by Capt. Jim Binkley, the Discovery looked different every summer as Binkley added two smokestacks, then decided one was more authentic, and installed picture windows and a walkway in addition to enlarging and lengthening the sternwheeler.

Upper left: Capt. Jim Binkley trains sons Johne and Skip in the wheelhouse. Upper right: Capt. Jim and Jim Jr. and one of the Titus youngsters from Minto looking on. Below: Discovery II, *rebuilt from the riverboat* Yutana, *was launched into the Chena River in 1971.*

By 1971, Binkley rebuilt the sternwheel freight boat *Yutana* into a second cruise boat with help from an old friend, Iver Johnson, and his step-father, Vince James. It became the 335-passenger *Discovery II,* which Binkley later enlarged in the early 1980s. The *Yutana* had traveled thousands of miles on the Yukon and its tributaries carrying bargeloads of freight to traders, trappers, miners, prospectors and Indian and Eskimo villages.

Clockwise starting with Capt. Jim Binkley, Johne, Marilee, Skip, Jim Jr. and Mary gathered for this family photo on the Discovery sternwheel in 1970.

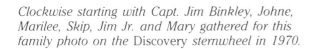

Civic Duty

Binkley also found time to work for Alaska Statehood, approved by Congress in 1958, and to serve two terms in the Alaska House of Representatives from 1961 to 1964—a path followed by son Johne who was elected in 1986 to a four-year term in the Alaska Senate after serving a term in the House. John Binkley's district is larger than the districts of most U.S. representatives and many U.S. senators.

Capt. Jim Binkley and his son Johne (above, with Rep. Al Adams of Kotzebue) also found time later to serve in the Alaska Legislature. Johne was elected to a 4-year term in the state Senate in 1986. His father served two terms in the state House of Representatives from 1961 to 1964.

During the winter of 1971-72, Jim Binkley and three other Alaskans, including his stepfather, built a sternwheeler, the *Canyon King*, from the ground up at Moab, Utah, for use on the nearby Colorado River. Binkley oversaw the design, gathered all the materials, and with his crew built the boat in 90 days.

Meanwhile, as tourism in Alaska grew and the *Discovery* cruises became one of the state's most popular attractions, the four Binkley children all

The Binkley clan gathers on the stern of Discovery II *in the early 1970s. By this time, all four children had assigned duties and responsibilities on the family's two sternwheelers.*

During the winter of 1972-73, Capt. Jim Binkley was commissioned by a operator named "Tex" McClatchy to build a sternwheeler in the Utah desert next to the Colorado River. The Canyon King *later was moved to Lake Powell where she is today.*

Skip Binkley, the eldest of the Binkley children, was the first to learn piloting from his father. Learning to handle a riverboat before he could drive a car, Skip at one time was the youngest licensed sternwheeler pilot in the United States.

assumed larger roles in the family's business, Alaska Riverways Inc.

Skip, Jim and Johne became riverboat pilots, learning to operate a sternwheeler before they could drive a car. "The Captain," as his family calls Jim Binkley, said Skip was a competent boat driver by the time he was 12 although he had to stand on a box to get the right view out the wheelhouse window. Once in a while someone would report seeing the sternwheeler coming down the Chena River with no pilot, Binkley recounts. Then the boat would swing around, glide up to the landing "and the wheelhouse door opened and a little kid walked out!"

The three boys also learned how to maintain the equipment, how to operate the boats and, with their sister, how to work with the crew. Promotion, advertising, sales and other facets of the family business are managed by Marilee, who also worked on the boats at an early age and now carries a significant part of the responsibility for the company.

Mary, meanwhile, is a Rock of Gibraltar in the family—a capable, competent helpmate and wife for Jim and a loving, caring mother and grandmother who instilled confidence in her children. She is physically small but as the Eskimos say, "Small but oh my!" A friend described her as an energetic, optimistic woman with a sincerity rarely seen. She treats passengers as if they were visitors coming into her own home.

Mary had studied anthropology at the nearby University of Alaska. Since the late 1950s, she has recruited scores of young Alaskan Indian and Eskimo students from villages throughout Alaska to serve as guides, sharing their culture at fish camps and villages visited by the *Discovery* sternwheelers.

Years later, the Binkleys found a way to honor the native cultures that had impressed Jim so much in his early days on the river. Under Jim Jr.'s direction, the family has created a repository for Athabascan and Eskimo culture on 25 acres of land near the turn-around point on their river cruise.

By 1986, with tourism expanding, a larger sternwheeler was needed to serve the growing demand. Jim and Mary Binkley already had six grandchildren and a seventh was on the way. The oldest grandchild was 8, already a junior deckhand. So the family decided to commission the 260-ton, 156-foot sternwheeler *Discovery III*. It was a decision made keeping in mind the 90 years of riverboating tradition that would be passed on to the rapidly expanding fourth generation of Binkleys: Ryan, Kai, Wade, James, Scott, Jon and Jacqueline.

There's more work to be done these days, but the Binkleys soak it up like a sponge. "It's a life out in the open air, and you get a lot of action. And it's a totally satisfying kind of business," said Capt. Jim Binkley, whose eyes light up when he talks about piloting on the river.

A big reason for the Binkleys' success is the satisfaction they feel sharing their heritage and their state with visitors.

"This legacy is being shared by so many people who are coming up for the same thing—the lure of Alaska," Binkley said. "It's a part of the Alaskan mystique."

With each trip on the river, he said, "You leave a little of yourself behind. The sharing is heartfelt. And we all love it.

"The motto in our family is that the greatest thing in life is to enjoy it. We're doing exactly what we want to do." ■

The Maiden Voyage
of *Discovery III*

"May your life span many generations and your decks be filled with happy visitors, and may your many sailings be safe ones as you symbolize the spirit of the early Alaskan pioneers—those qualities of adventure, dedication and discovery. With love I christen the *Discovery III*."

With those words, Mary Binkley, spritely matriarch of the Binkleys, broke the traditional bottle of champagne over a capstan at the bow, christening the *Discovery III* on May 9, 1987.

Capt. Jim Binkley, surrounded by Mary and the couple's four children and their families, Skip and Karen, Jim Jr. and DMae, Johne and Judy, and Marilee and her fiance, George "Buzz" Faulhaber, declared the new boat to be "the most sophisticated sternwheel riverboat ever built."

The sternwheeler was a distillation of the Binkley experience and represented the family's hopes for the future. Powered by twin 540-horsepower diesel engines, she has bow-thrusters, stern-thrusters, a unique adjustable contravane in front of the paddlewheel, hydraulic drive system, four depth-sounders, a complete radio and sophisticated on-board sound system, and a half-dozen video cameras with monitors forward and aft to keep an eye on things as well as provide a monitor for the passengers. The

Mary Binkley and granddaughter Kai (above) enjoy the festivities surrounding the christening of Discovery III *in May, 1987. Capt. Jim and Mary (right) prepare to break the traditional bottle of champagne over a capstan on the bow.*

Visitors industry representatives ride on a wing bridge next to the wheelhouse with Seattle's skyline in the background.

the big boat to her home port in Fairbanks. Back home, the rest of the family prepared for the 38th season of river cruises.

After Coast Guard certification, tests and sea trials on Puget Sound, the sternwheeler was loaded onto a Knappton Corp. barge for the 3,500-mile trip across the Gulf of Alaska and around the Alaska Peninsula into the Bering Sea and finally to St. Marys near the mouth of the Yukon River.

At last, in her own element, *Discovery III* was ready for her maiden voyage. ◼

72-inch steering wheel came from the steamer *Yukon*, a sternwheeler built in Whitehorse, Y.T., in 1913.

Built of lightweight steel that was specially poured in an Oregon steel mill, her 260 tons could float in 3 feet of water.

After the christening at Langley, Wash., the Binkleys took aboard nearly 700 shipyard workers and their spouses, transplanted Alaskans, retired sternwheeler pilots and captains, and movers and shakers in the Northwest tourist industry for a 2½-hour cruise on Puget Sound. Most of the passengers wore turn-of-the-century costumes.

For Skip Binkley, who supervised the construction, one major chore remained—delivering

Capt. Jim Binkley answers questions at an impromptu news conference during a news media cruise aboard Discovery III *near Seattle.*

The Yutana Barge Lines tug Pastolik *pushes the barge that brought* Discovery III *to St. Marys near the mouth of the Yukon River.*

Heading up the Yukon

At St. Marys, a Yupik Eskimo fishing village on the Yukon Delta, water is pumped into airtight compartments built into the barge that brought the 156-foot sternwheeler from Seattle. It is a tricky operation because the barge must sink evenly to prevent the Discovery III from tipping over.

Two days after the operation begins, a sense of freedom and exhilaration sweeps the big boat as she floats freely and begins her maiden run nearly 1,000 miles up the Yukon, Tanana and Chena rivers to Fairbanks.

Tuesday, June 23, 1987
10 a.m. —Barge carrying *Discovery III* arrives in St. Marys.

Billy Beans, 80, a short, husky man hardened by a lifetime of fishing and trapping, smiles broadly as he recalls the old steamboats once so important on the Yukon River.

"The *Sarah . . . Louise . . . Suzie.*" He is reciting a litany of the steamboat trade.

Beans, like many others in this green, hilly village of about 500 people, has come down to the dock to watch a Yutana Barge Lines crew unload a sternwheeler from the oceangoing barge that brought her from Puget Sound. Word

gets around quickly: *Discovery III* is heading for Fairbanks, the first sternwheeler to make the trip in more than 30 years.

Beans is a respected Yupik Eskimo elder in St. Marys who consents to a midnight interview following the Tuesday night bingo game. The interview takes place on a high hill overlooking the dark Andreafsky River and the Yukon delta beyond. The Yukon River is a ribbon on the

Three youngsters ham it up at St. Marys where villagers come watch the unloading of the first sternwheeler to make the trip upriver in 30 years.

St. Marys has more all-terrain vehicles than cars and trucks.

Much of the building material in this treeless delta is salvaged from the river, and one or two weather-worn cabins appear to embrace a few bones of the old steamboats abandoned here more than half a century ago. Across the Andreafsky River, parts of steamboat boilers and the metal skeleton of a paddlewheel stick out of the water, a haven for gulls and a reminder of a time gone by.

horizon. From beyond the hills behind us a low-lying sun projects shades of pink.

This elderly gentleman owes his very name to the steamboats that once ruled this big river. He loves to retell the story of his father, a pilot, making a long run to Canada one season on a sternwheeler that nearly exhausted its food supplies. Finally there was nothing left but beans.

Once day, Beans said, his father was standing relief at the wheel while the captain ate. "And when they come up from eating, he always tell my dad, 'All right Capt. Beans, time for you to go down to have your beans.' He call him Capt. Beans. That's how we got our name. That name stick.

"You go down to Mountain Village and you hear nothing but Beans names—Beans, Beans, Beans!" He shakes with laughter at the thought.

He remembers when people of the lower Yukon earned money from the steamboats, serving as deckhands, collecting and chopping driftwood.

This little girl wasn't certain she wanted her picture taken but momma said it was alright.

Pieces of an old steamboat boiler stick out of the water on a slough of the Andreafsky River near St. Marys.

Johne Binkley and son, Ryan, 8, ride ahead in the "sounder boat" as Discovery III *leaves St. Marys.*

Wednesday, June 24
4:05 p.m. —Barge decks awash but not enough to float *Discovery III*.

Because the barge holding the *Discovery III* has begun to sink unevenly, its forward port side hung up on a rock or sandbar on the bottom, a decision is made to refloat the barge partially, pull it farther out into the river and try again.

This is a traditional method of moving shallow-draft riverboats and it requires patience.

Edwin L. Lindbeck, a grandfatherly gentleman from Anchorage, is a marine surveyor who has come alive with this complication. Representing a consortium of insurance companies that have insured this new multimillion dollar stern-wheeler, Lindbeck counsels a slow and careful approach.

For another 24 hours, the pumps drone on as water is removed from more than a dozen watertight compartments in the barge. Refloated, the barge is moved a short distance into deeper water and the slow process of sinking the barge—a delicate balancing act—begins again.

Thursday, June 25
4 p.m. —Free of barge.
10:45 p.m. —Passed Pilot Station.

Exhilaration and a sense of freedom sweep *Discovery III* as she runs up the Andreafsky River to take on 2,000 gallons of fresh water, then whistles a farewell passing St. Marys en route to the Yukon a few miles below. Finally we are on the Yukon—wide, silent, serene. The vastness is overpowering.

Skip Binkley, 38, and his brother, Johne, 34, are sharing command of this high-tech riverboat. The brothers are third-generation riverboatmen, both licensed pilots. Eight-year-old Ryan, Johne's son, is a junior deckhand and fourth-generation Binkley on the Yukon.

Friday, June 26
5:10 a.m. —Marshall
2:45 p.m. —Russian Mission
11 p.m. —Paimuit

Sunshine and clouds combine to project intricate designs on the bare flanks of green and purple hills to the north.

The steady churning of the red, 20-foot paddle-wheel seems in tune with the history of the

The lower Yukon is wide, silent and serene. The vastness is overpowering.

steamboat era as we follow early trade routes, rising from Yupik villages near the coast to Athabascan Indian villages of the Interior.

Steamboats had explored and traded on the 1,990-mile Yukon River since Alaska's purchase from Russia in 1867. But it was the Klondike Gold Rush of 1898 that brought on the heyday of the steamboats.

Saturday, June 27
4 a.m. —Holy Cross
10 a.m. —Anvik
1 p.m. —Grayling

"We're in God's country now," Dave Walker, 70, of Holy Cross, announces over coffee in the

Anton Charlie of Grayling, who says he's "about 90, I guess."

Nellie Wharton, 79, Elma Nicholas, 86, and Leni Dementi, 81, recall the old steamboats.

The Nenana, *a Yutana Barges Lines tug, pushes two barges upriver near Ruby.*

Children gathered on the riverbank at Nulato to watch the Discovery III *pass by.*

galley as we move into the Yukon highlands.

Walker's name commands respect on the river. He is a river pilot brought out of retirement to assist the Binkleys on this maiden voyage. Walker has been a pilot for 50 years and not only knows every bend and island in the river, but also seems to have a story to go with each one. He's a walking encyclopedia about the Yukon and its history, people and points of interest.

Walker chuckles at romanticized notions of the steamboat era.

"The oldtimers talk about the 'good old days' but it was nothing but hard work you know," he said. "Really, and those old steamers burning wood, and packing freight out on your back—100 pounds of flour and spuds and all that. You had no kind of equipment to (help you) unload."

Walker's grandfather was a Scotsman who hiked the Chilkoot Trail during the Klondike Gold Rush. His grandmother was part Atha-

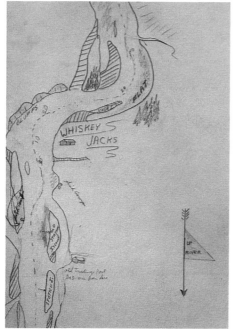

A page from Dave Walker's hand-drawn river map.

bascan, French Canadian and Russian. His father was an independent operator who ran a 30-foot barge up and down the Innoko and Iditarod rivers, both Yukon tributaries. That's where Walker learned to read the river.

In Grayling, a village of 220 people, four elders sit on a wooden bench overlooking the river.

Belle Deacon, 83, of Anvik, and a few of her friends, including Nellie Wharton, 79, Elma Nicholas, 86, and Leni Dementi, 81, remember the old steamers.

They all talk at once, their fragile voices a sweet litany.

"One is *Sarah*, one is *Suzie*, one is *Jacob* . . . *Julia*. And there's . . . *Jeff Davis*, *Julia B* . . . *Reliance*. . . There was lots of big boats . . . *Alice*. Oh yes, *Alice*."

Sunday, June 28
9:10 a.m. —Kaltag
2:50 p.m. —Nulato
5:30 p.m. —Koyukuk
7:50 p.m. —Bishop Rock

The *Discovery III* is following the first of the salmon runs upriver. Already the orange-red strips of fish are hanging on racks to dry as the fish camps, smoke houses and fishwheels come to life.

In Nulato, the beach is crowded with flat-bottom riverboats, fish nets and all-terrain vehicles. An army of children turn out to watch *Discovery III* go by.

Crispin Esmailka, 69, a former deckhand, remembers the enormous amount of wood consumed by the steamboats.

Coming upriver after a trip to Marshall on the lower Yukon, he recalls the steamer *Nenana* filling a barge with more than 400 cords of wood. En route to her home port in Nenana, the steamer unloaded 15 to 20 cords every 20 or 30 miles on the Tanana River where wood was hard to find.

"I used to know a lot of guys who had camps here and there, cutting wood," Esmailka said. "You used to cut wood by contracts. Some would get a 50-cord contract, or 100 cords, or 30—whatever they think they could cut over the winter."

Monday, June 29
11 p.m. —Arrive Galena. Take on water and fuel.

Discovery III whistles a greeting to about 500 Galena residents and visitors who have come to the riverbank with their children, dogs and all-terrain vehicles.

"That's the sound of the Yukon," somebody yells enthusiastically from the crowd.

A yellow tail-dragger airplane buzzes the sternwheeler, and small riverboats circle for a better view as *Discovery III* edges to the landing on Front Street. Flash photography punctuates the near-midnight dusk.

Discovery III stops at this Yukon-Koyukuk supply center for fuel and fresh water—plus a bit of politics.

This stop has turned into a major event and it's mostly Johne Binkley's show. Binkley is a state senator from this region.

"Come on aboard," Binkley yells to the crowd from the top of the gangplank and nearly 300 people noisily file on for a free 45-minute ride upriver.

Free rides
at midnight

After running virtually non-stop for five days, Discovery III made a stop for fuel at Galena, an important Yukon-Koyukuk supply center. An offer of free rides was radioed ahead and despite the midnight hour, nearly 300 villagers happily climbed aboard for a 45-minute cruise up the river and back.

Crewman Neil MacKinnon explores Kokrines, now abandoned but once one of the largest Athabascan villages on the Yukon River.

Tuesday, June 30
2 a.m. —Depart Galena.
10:33 a.m. —Ruby

The Yukon is deep and narrower, wedged between high emerald hills, as we pass Ruby, an historic mining town. A crew member returns from the village with a freshly caught salmon for dinner.

There is camaraderie and routine on board now.

With two stopwatches, cook and deckhand Don Dryden and Skip Binkley measure the movement of small wood blocks from bow to stern, calculating *Discovery III* is making 9.3 knots, or 10.6 mph, against the current. Less current, we are making about 5 miles per hour, as expected.

Life aboard the boat—including meals—is organized along 6-hour watches with a pilot, engineer and deckhand on duty at all times.

Most of the crew slept in tents on the boiler deck.

Life aboard the boat is organized in 6-hour watches in which a pilot, engineer and deckhand run the boat.

Most of the activity takes place in and around the galley on the main deck. Next up, the boiler deck offers a 360-degree view through picture windows in weatherproof comfort. Above is the exposed weather deck—great for photography—and a few steps higher, the Texas deck, covered but open on the sides. The wheelhouse is large, quiet and comfortable— "like the cockpit of a 747," said Skip Binkley.

Meanwhile, crewman Kenny Persinger has installed a portable shower complete with hot and cold running water on the fantail next to the wheel.

The shower stall is open to the stern and has no top. Cool mist from the roaring sternwheel floats down as the view unwinds. Ah, life on the river!

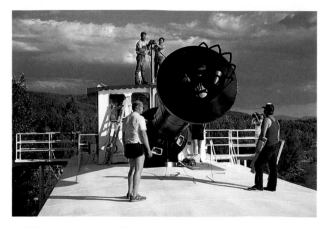

Wednesday, July 1
8:20 a.m. —Tanana
9:40 p.m. —Manley Hot Springs

There is excitement and a trace of tension in the wheelhouse as we turn into the Tanana River. Skip Binkley decides to fall in behind the *Tanana*, a Yutana Barge Lines tug pushing a barge, in search of the elusive Tanana channel.

The Tanana River is shallower, narrower and faster than the Yukon, and its main channel is unpredictable and often hard to find. Its channels shift frequently during the season, sometimes overnight, and a pilot's map of the river is outdated quickly.

"Hey, we just touched bottom," Skip Binkley reports as we nudge a buildup of silt and sand near the mouth of the river.

Ahead, a "sounder boat" from the tug and barge crosses back and forth, looking for the channel. For miles, the river winds lazily through the wide flatland with its vast sandbars, half-moon sloughs and abandoned riverbeds.

This is the first shallow-water test for the riverboat designed specifically with the Tanana River in mind. Drawing less than 3 feet, she passes with flying colors.

The sternwheeler pulls up to the bank downriver from Nenana.

Would she fit under Nenana's railroad bridge —just barely!

The Binkleys had planned for this moment—moving Discovery III *under the Alaska Railroad bridge at Nenana. The wheelhouse sits approximately 43 feet out of the water. The stack, another 11 feet, had been built on hinges just in case.*

"We've looked at water measurements here for the last 20 years at this time, and in 95 percent of the time, the water level was low enough," Skip Binkley said.

After stopping a few bends below Nenana, the stack is lowered and crewman Rocky MacDonald slaps the lower steel girder on the bridge as the sternwheeler inches under the bridge.

Thursday, July 2
9 p.m. —Passed under Nenana bridges.

Edmund Lord, a big man, is sitting broadly on a newly built fishwheel a couple bends below Nenana. He once served as a cook and deckhand on the *Kusko*, the 35-foot propeller boat owned by Art Peterson that carried mail to the upper Yukon regions before World War II.

Capt. Jim Binkley, then a young man, was one of the *Kusko* crew and Lord remembers the day Binkley gave him first aid after an accident left him with a severely cut thumb.

"He saved my thumb and it's still working good," he said, waving a thumb with its neatly stitched scar.

And from Nora Lord comes the litany of the river: "Steamer *Nenana, Jacob, Alice, Yukon . . .*"

A crowd gathers on the riverbank to watch as the Binkley crew winches down the sternwheeler's smokestack, which sits 43 feet on top of the water. Built on hinges, it must come down so that the boat can clear the Alaska Railroad bridge at Nenana.

Half an hour later, crewman Rocky MacDonald rests on his haunches atop the wheelhouse, slapping the lowermost steel girder on the black bridge, as the boat inches under.

Crew members tend to the "sounder boat" used to take depth soundings in shallow water.

Discovery III *approaches Fairbanks on a hot, brilliantly sunny July day.*

A Tanana River sunset is photographed within 10 minutes of midnight on the last night of the maiden voyage.

Friday, July 3
2:42 p.m. —Fairbanks

Skip Binkley executes that familiar sharp turn into the Chena River on a hot, brilliantly sunny afternoon, attracting riverboats, airplanes and riverbank crowds.

The new sternwheeler is home. Champagne materializes on ice in the galley. The trip is over for the six crew members and three passengers who left St. Marys six days and 22 hours before.

A relieved Skip Binkley, whose heavy responsibilities began with the keel-laying the previous October, says he's "glad to have it done."

"But I know I'm going to look back on it with fond memories," he adds. ∎

As Discovery III *arrives at her Fairbanks landing, the older sternwheelers look small in this view from the wheelhouse.*

Rocky MacDonald (left) opens a bottle of champagne to celebrate safe arrival of Discovery III. *Capt. Jim Binkley and grandson Jon (above) share a happy moment.*

Capt. Jim Binkley gives away his daughter, Marilee, in marriage at a gala wedding aboard newly arrived Discovery III.

Take the tour and a short course in Alaska history

Cruising down the Chena and Tanana rivers with Capt. Jim and Mary Binkley is like signing up for a short course on Alaskana. You ought to be getting college credits.

On any given summer day, the narration will cover interesting sights along the river and a generous amount of Alaska history and culture as well as anthropology, paleontology, upper atmospheric physics, geology, botany, biology, glaciology, hydrology, mining, engineering, economics, public affairs and plenty of humor—all of which Capt. Binkley describes as "a spring-board to other subjects."

After four decades of answering questions from visitors, there aren't many questions these pioneer Alaskans can't answer. But just in case, there's a two-way radio in the wheelhouse and Jim has been known to track down an expert at the nearby University of Alaska Fairbanks when the rare question comes along that he can't answer.

A sampling from Jim and Mary's fascinating commentary delivered aboard their sternwheeler cruises:

Mary Binkley and a guide show off Indian beadwork and fur pelts.

Mary Shields and friend watch the departing Discovery III *after a stop on the Tanana River.*

ATHABASCANS. United by their language, more North American Indians speak Athabascan than any other Indian language. Approximately 200,000 Athabascans extend as far as the west side of Hudson Bay and as far south as New Mexico and Arizona, where the Navajos and Apaches are Athabascans who speak basically the same language and are believed to have shared a common ancestor who crossed the Bering land bridge 10,000 to 12,000 years ago.

BUSH PLANES. Alaska's small "bush" planes are versatile. Many are equipped with balloon tires, or "tundra tires" as some pilots call them, for landing on sand and gravel bars. Some are equipped with pontoons for water landings in the summer, then are lifted out of the water in the fall and the floats replaced with skis. Approximately one out of every 40 Alaskans is a licensed pilot, more than any other state.

CHENA. This little town on the Tanana River about 14 miles from Fairbanks was founded in 1902. It competed jealously with Fairbanks to attract population and seemed to be winning in its first four years, growing to approximately 2,000 people. It had docks for riverboats that often could not get up the Chena River to Fairbanks. By 1906, however, it became apparent Fairbanks had more political clout, attracting the U.S. jail, District Court and other government offices. Completion of the Alaska Railroad in 1923 to Fairbanks was the final blow. Many of the buildings were pulled to Fairbanks on the river ice by horses and today little remains of Chena.

CHENA RIVER. An Athabascan Indian name meaning "game river or good hunting river," the Chena is a spring-fed river originating about 90 miles east of Fairbanks, draining approximately 2,000 square miles and reaching its maximum flow during April and May from spring rains and breakup. The Chena runs at its lowest level in September, except in 1967 when three weeks of August rain flooded Fairbanks with 2 to 5 feet of muddy water. The Chena empties into the Tanana River 12 miles downriver from downtown Fairbanks.

CLIMATE. Interior Alaska is semi-arid and receives about 8 to 13 inches of annual precipitation including snowfall. It has wide temperature swings, as high as 100 degrees, as low as 72 below. Fairbanks receives little wind. In winter, the air has virtually no moisture. You'll never encounter anything so dry. You must hydrate your house to keep your furniture from loosening up. Talk about static electricity: One is constantly grounding away the static charge through a finger or knuckle against some object. You come into the house in the evening and when you cross the rug to greet your spouse with a good-evening kiss, you'd better hold hands first or you'll really pucker up! The school children may stay home if the temperature drops below minus 50 degrees.

DOG MUSHING. Sled dog racing is Alaska's favorite sport, both long-distance events and "sprint" races in which dog teams are run over relatively short distances in two- or three-day timed "heats." Major events each winter and early spring include the World Championship Sled Dog Race in Anchorage and the North American Sled Dog Championship in Fairbanks (both sprint races) and two distance races of more than 1,000 miles—the Iditarod Sled Dog Race from Anchorage to Nome and the Yukon Quest International between Fairbanks and Whitehorse, Y.T.

FISHWHEELS. A floating fish trap often fabricated of white spruce logs and poles, the fishwheel consists of two baskets on either side of a wooden axle that dip in and out of the water, turned by the current. After migrating salmon are caught in the basket, the fish drop into a wooden trough, then slide into a catch box. Anthropologists say the fishwheel was introduced by an early settler near the confluence of the Chena and Tanana rivers about 1904 and since then have become widely used for subsistence fishing.

GEOGRAPHY. Fairbanks lies at 64 degrees north, 100 miles below the Arctic Circle, 1,800 miles south of the North Pole, 60 minutes away from the Soviet Union if you boarded a passenger jet and flew west. The tip of the Aleutian Chain extends to within 1,000 miles of Japan, and it's as far across Alaska as it is from Savannah, Georgia, to San Francisco. The United States bought this vast territory from Russia in 1867 for $7.2 million. What a deal!

Fishwheels and fish camps come to life in the Yukon River drainage as the first waves of salmon migrate upriver to spawn.

Patsy Aamodt of Barrow and Flora Bergman of Allakaket worked as guides aboard the Discovery in 1971. Bergman went on to become Miss Eskimo Olympics.

GILL NETS. White floats on top of the water indicate the presence of a gill net which hangs down like a curtain, catching the salmon that swim into it. Under state fish and game regulations, Alaskans are entitled to take a certain number of fish each year—for personal consumption only, not for resale.

INDIAN SURVIVAL CAMP. The Indians are concerned about the loss of their culture. The elders bring young Indian children to this camp on the Tanana River and keep them for one to two weeks, teaching them about their culture. They'll teach them some of their language, the songs and dances, and tell them stories and legends around the campfire. Then they'll teach them to track animals and how to live in harmony with nature. The kids love it.

MT. MCKINLEY. At 20,320 feet North America's highest peak, Mt. McKinley has a little deck of clouds around the top a good part of the year. The winds have to blow hard at the upper altitude to disperse them. In Alaska, Mt. McKinley is widely known and officially designated as "Denali," an Indian word meaning "the great one." The mountain is part of the Alaska Range, which in the last 40 million years was formed, eroded and formed again, leaving some 2,000 feet of glacial debris under the Tanana Valley.

NATIVE PEOPLES. The Aleuts live mostly in the Aleutian Chain, the Eskimos generally live in the Arctic and along the western and northern coasts and the Indians live in the Interior, in Southcentral Alaska in the Panhandle.

NORTHERN LIGHTS. Also known as the Aurora Borealis, the northern lights are a spectacular natural phenomenon seen in the Arctic skies most frequently in October and April. The eerie flicking bands of lights are created when charged electrons and protons—unleashed from sunspots—strike gas particles in the upper atmosphere.

PERMAFROST. Permafrost is ground that has remained frozen for more than two years. It can be a serious problem for the Alaskan who builds a home on it only to watch the home sink when the disturbed ground begins to melt. In Arctic Alaska, many structures are built above the ground so as not to disturb the permafrost.

SALMON MIGRATION. The salmon migrate upriver to lay their eggs and die in the same river where they were spawned. Ordinarily, the fish can't tolerate the silt in a glacier river but there is enough oxygen in the Tanana provided from the freshwater tributaries to see them along their way. Three species of salmon—kings, chums and silvers—are found in the Tanana watershed.

SMOKED SALMON. How to make mouth-watering smoked salmon: Cut the fish into small chunks, glaze with a brine solution that includes brown sugar and honey, smoke at 105 degrees with alder smoke for 12 hours, exactly. That's the most delicious smoked salmon you've ever had in your life.

TREES. Interior Alaska's most common trees are willow, aspen, birch, balsam poplar, alder, tamarack and two species of evergreen: the white spruce and black spruce. The white spruce, commonly used in home construction, grows to an average 19-22 inches in diameter requiring approximately 170 years of growth to reach that size.

QIVIUT. An Eskimo word meaning down, qiviut is the underwool of the musk oxen grown during the winter months. Alaska has one domestic herd near Palmer which provides qiviut for a cottage industry in the Kuskokwim-Yukon area where Eskimos hand-knit hats, scarves and stoles which are softer than cashmere and eight times warmer than sheep's wool.

TANANA RIVER. The Tanana is not only one of the Yukon River's largest tributaries, it is also the largest glacier-fed stream in the world, carrying 100,000 tons of "glacier dust" or "glacier flour" past Fairbanks every day to the Bering Sea, 1,250 miles downriver. The pure glacier water is turned brown by the silt of more than 100 glaciers, which over millions of years will flatten a rocky mountain down to a field of powder like your kitchen flour. The Tanana's channels are shifting constantly, forming new sandbars, eroding the banks and forming sloughs. If we get stuck on a sandbar, anyone over 3 feet tall is going to have to get out and push! ■

An all-terrain vehicle and an outboard riverboat are important forms of transportation for subsistence fishermen catching salmon during the annual runs.

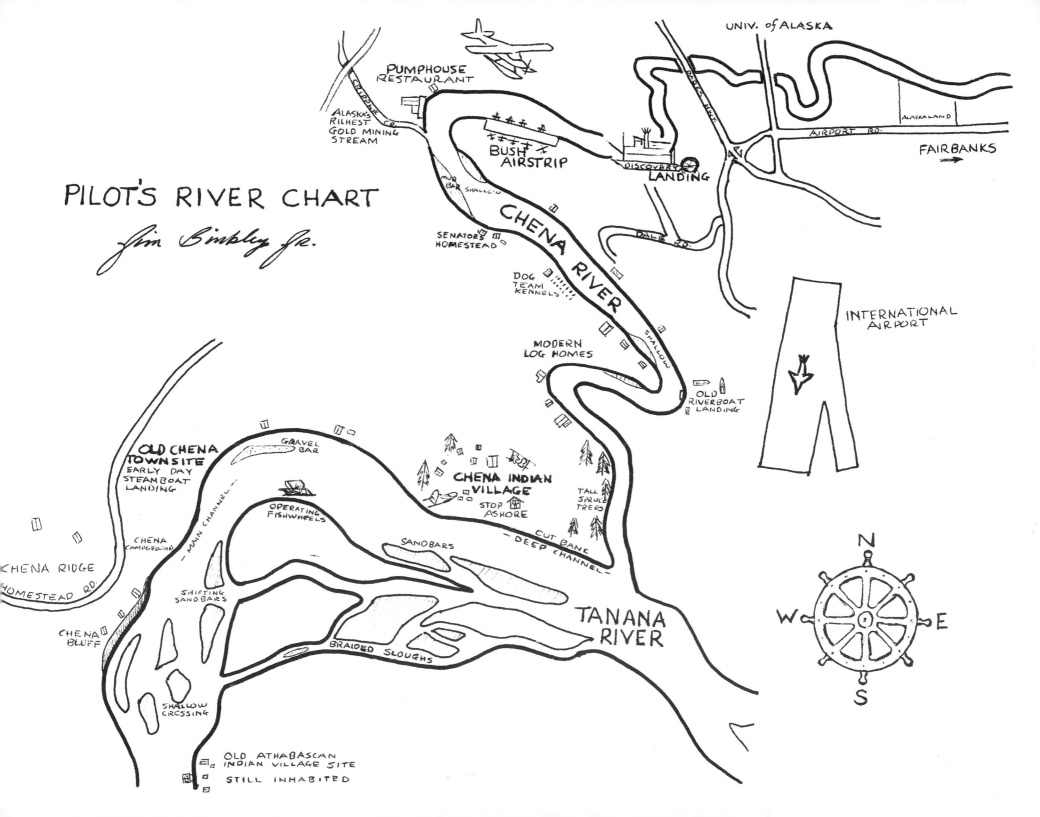

Those Binkley Boats

Charlie Binkley, his son Jim, and grand-children have built and served on more than three dozen boats over four generations. Here is a partial list of them:

Bailey—Charlie Binkley worked on this 193-ton sternwheeler, built at Lake Bennett in 1899, the first season after arriving in the Klondike. The *Bailey* ran from Lake Bennett to Canyon City during the gold rush, and later operated between Whitehorse to Dawson.

Seattle Spirit—Charlie, his half-brother Emerson Reid and a syndicate of investors won the 10-meter class in the Pacific Coast Championship with this sleek boat in the summer of 1910. In July, the *Seattle Spirit*, designed and built by Binkley, made a 30-mile run at an average of 32.4 miles per hour and was believed to be the fastest boat on the West Coast.

Wigwam—Another speed boat raced by Charlie Binkley and Emerson Reid. The *Wigwam* and the two brothers were featured on the cover of the July, 1912, *Pacific Motor Boat.*

B&B Nos. 1, 2, 3 and 4—Built by Charlie Binkley and Sid Barrington at the mouth of Ship Creek near the new city of Anchorage. The boats moved men and supplies upriver for construction of the Alaska Railroad between 1914-16.

Hazel B—A series of riverboats that revolutionized the river trade upriver from Wrangell on the Stikine River, run by Sid Barrington and Charlie Binkley, who designed and built many of them.

Hazel B No. 1—Built at Dawson between 1908-10, this riverboat was operated by Sid Barrington and Charlie Binkley on the Yukon River.

Hazel B No. 1 (second with this name)—Built by Jim Binkley's uncle, Emerson Reid, this 64-foot riverboat was launched in Wrangell in 1941. She was brought north from the Stikine River for military work in World War II, during which Jim Binkley served as a pilot.

Hazel B No. 2—An 88-foot twin-screw tunnel boat built in Anchorage in 1916 by Charlie Binkley and Sid Barrington for use on the Susitna River during Alaska Railroad construction. She was converted to a fish saltery in Southeast Alaska after the 1917 season.

Hazel B No. 2 (second with this name)—Designed by Charlie Binkley, this 90-foot tunnel-sterned propeller boat was launched in Wrangell in 1925. She was destroyed by fire in 1932.

Hazel B No. 2 (third with this name)—This continuation of the *Hazel B* series, built after Charlie Binkley's death, drew only 20 inches of water fully loaded. The Army renamed her the *ST467* and Jim Binkley commanded the vessel for two years during World War II.

Hazel B No. 3—Designed and built by Charlie Binkley at Wrangell in 1917, this 62-foot, 95-horsepower gasoline-powered boat, reported to run in water as shallow as 9 inches, made the run to Telegraph Creek in a record 26 hours on her maiden voyage up the Stikine River.

Hazel B No. 4—Designed and built by Charlie Binkley, this 65-foot, 100-horsepower gasoline-powered riverboat was launched at Wrangell in 1919 for service on the Stikine.

The Hazel B No. 3, *built by Charlie Binkley at Wrangell in 1917, made the run up the Stikine River to Telegraph Creek in a record 26 hours on her maiden voyage.*

Kusko—The 35-foot *Kusko* was operated by Art Peterson, George Black's son-in-law, as a mail and military cargo boat in the early 1940s with Jim aboard as deckhand and pilot.

Idler—Jim also worked as a deckhand and pilot aboard this 62-foot riverboat built by the Noyes family in Fairbanks about 1910. After it lay in Noyes Slough for many years, George Black bought the *Idler*, converting it from a steamboat to a diesel with a chain-driven sternwheel. It was aboard this boat that Jim Binkley got his first sternwheeler experience as Black carried freight and passengers on the Yukon River and its tributaries.

Mudhen—A small tugboat, measuring about 30 feet long, operated by George Black in the early 1940s.

Danako No. 1—Jim Binkley was a pilot aboard this diesel-powered tunnel boat that drew just 18 inches of water. Operated by Clyde Day of Day Navigation Co., she and her barges ran up shallow side streams off the Yukon River.

Elaine G—Jim Binkley was a pilot for several trips aboard this diesel sternwheeler operated by Don Peterson during the war.

Aksala—This 642-ton sternwheeler was built at Whitehorse in 1913 and named the *Alaska* by its original owner, the Alaska Yukon Navigation Co. During the war, Jim Binkley was a pilot aboard this sternwheeler leased by Sid Barrington from British Yukon Navigation, which had renamed it the *Aksala*.

Klondike II—Jim Binkley served briefly aboard this British Yukon Navigation Co. sternwheeler as an American pilot assigned by the U.S. Army. This riverboat was built in Whitehorse in 1937. Among other assignments, the *Klondike* pushed bargeloads of equipment for construction of military facilities.

Alice II—Capt. Bill Mackey, a Finn, was skipper aboard this old wood-burning sternwheeler when Jim Binkley served briefly as a military pilot. During the 1940s, the *Alice* carried the Alaska Railroad's freight and passengers on the Tanana and Yukon rivers. The 262-ton riverboat was built in Seattle in 1909 for the Northern Commercial Co.

Barry K—Originally named the *Lewiston* and operated by the Union Pacific Railroad on the Columbia and Snake rivers, this 160-foot wooden-hulled sternwheeler was bought by the Army on the Columbia River for use in Alaska during World War II. She was built in 1923. Jim Binkley made several trips as pilot aboard the *Barry K*.

Capt. Jim Binkley carried passengers and freight on the Yukon River between Circle City and Fort Yukon aboard the Pelican *in the late 1950s.*

Taku Chief—Originally built for the Taku River in Southeast Alaska, the twin-screw, shallow-draft tug was brought to Interior Alaska by the former Civil Aeronautics Administration. Jim Binkley was a pilot aboard the *Taku Chief* for a time during 1948.

Godspeed—Jim and Mary Binkley bought this boat from the Episcopal Church in 1950 at the urging of Chuck West, a Wien Air Lines pilot who had flown the Hump during World War II. West recognized the tourism potential of Alaska and was seeking ways to entertain and thrill the early tour groups he brought to Fairbanks.

Skookum—Jim Binkley bought this military surplus motor vessel from Jimmy Huntington for $500. After virtually rebuilding the tug from the hull up and adding twin diesel engines, Binkley ran his own Yukon River freighting operation in the early 1950s.

Pelican—Built in Seattle by Norman Blanchard in 1932 for the Episcopal bishop in Alaska, she was about 60 feet long and 10 feet abeam. Her single screw, powered by a gas engine, gave her lots of speed. She had beautiful lines but a draft deeper than most riverboats. Later, she was converted to diesel and worked with the *Kusko* and *Idler*. Bill English and Jim Binkley bought the vessel from George Black's estate and used her to haul passengers and freight between Circle City and Fort Yukon for a few years before Alaska statehood in 1959. *Discovery* passengers view this boat at the old shipyard on the Chena River.

Capt. Jim Binkley was a pilot aboard the Taku Chief *(top) operated by the Army during World War II. Binkley operated two other boats, the* Skookum *and the* Pelican *(above) about the time of Alaska statehood in 1959.*

Capt. Jim Binkley built this little sternwheeler from the ground up in 1955 in his back yard on Noyes Slough near Fairbanks.

Discovery—Jim Binkley and Bill English were partners in this sternwheeler Binkley built from the ground up in his back yard on Noyes Slough in 1955. Over the years, he lengthened it twice, increasing the capacity from 49 to 150.

Gypsy—This handsome 90-footer, a sailboat converted to a motor vessel, once was used by actor John Barrymore in Mexican waters. In 1959, Jim Binkley found this boat in Newport Beach, Calif., for a group of Alaskans planning to offer summer passenger service and glacier cruises in Prince William Sound. En route from California to Seattle, Binkley and his small crew rescued two men caught in a small outboard in a fierce storm.

Discovery II—The Binkleys' second stern-wheeler started life as the *Yutana,* a riverboat owned by Capt. George Black, who later fell off the vessel and drowned in the early 1950s. At one time the *Yutana* served as a ferry at Nenana before construction of the Parks Highway Bridge. Jim Binkley had worked briefly on the *Yutana* before he bought it and made an extensive conversion for use as a sternwheel cruise boat.

Canyon King—Jim Binkley and a three-man crew from Fairbanks built this sternwheeler in the Utah desert the winter of 1972-73. The job took 90 days and the *Canyon King* later plied both the Colorado River and Lake Powell in Arizona. She's still operating on Lake Powell.

Discovery III—This 156-foot sternwheeler designed by the Binkleys and engineered by Bill Preston was launched on Puget Sound in 1987 and brought 4,500 miles to Fairbanks.

During the winter of 1972-73, Capt. Jim Binkley and several other Alaskans went to Utah where they built a sternwheeler, the Canyon King, *from scratch in 90 days for use on the Colorado River.*

Bibliography

Alaska Almanac, The, Alaska Northwest Publishing Co., Edmonds, Wash., 1986.

Alaska Wilderness Milepost, Alaska Northwest Publishing Co., Edmonds, Wash., 1986.

Anderson, Barry C., *Lifeline to the Yukon: A History of Yukon River Navigation*, Superior Publishing Co., Seattle, 1983.

Atwood, Evangeline, *Anchorage: All-American City*, Binfords and Mort, Portland, 1957.

Clifford, Howard, *Rails North, The Railroads of Alaska and the Yukon*, Superior Publishing Co., Seattle, 1981.

Cole, Terrence, *E.T. Barnette: The Strange Story of the Man Who Founded Fairbanks*, Alaska Northwest Publishing Co., Edmonds, Wash., 1981.

Gary, John T. and Rowe, J. Phillip, *An Alaska Census of Transportation*, Institute of Social and Economic Research, University of Alaska, 1982.

Hedrick, Basil and Savage, Susan, *Steamboats on the Chena: The Founding and Development of Fairbanks, Alaska*, Epicenter Press, Fairbanks, 1988.

Kitchener, L.D., *Flag over the North*, Superior Publishing Co., Seattle, 1954.

Knutson, Arthur E., *Sternwheels on the Yukon*, Knutson Enterprises, Inc., Kirkland, Wash., 1970.

Matheson, Janet, *Fairbanks: A City Historical Building Survey*, City of Fairbanks, 1985.

Pacific Motor Boat magazine, Seattle, 1910-13.

Seattle Post-Intelligencer, Seattle, Wash., July, 1897.

Stikine River, The, Alaska Geographic Society, Anchorage, 1979.

Yukon River Steamboats: a Pictorial History, Pictorial Histories Publishing Co., Missoula, Mont., 1982.

Wrangell Sentinel, Wrangell, 1915-1925.

Discovery III's impressive statistics:
Length overall . . . . 156 feet
Length of hull . . . . 132 feet
Beam . . . . 34 feet
Gross weight . . . . 260 tons
Draft . . . . .3 feet
Power . . . . two 540-hp diesels
Passengers 1,000

Photo credits

Color photos by Kent Sturgis, black and white photos from the Binkley family collection and as otherwise credited: Page 10, photos courtesy of Kay Guthrie & Associates; Page 11, photo courtesy of Nichols Bros. Boat Builders; Pages 18-21, photo archives, Alaska and Polar Regions Department, University of Alaska; Page 22, lower photo, ibid; Page 24, ibid; Page 27, ibid; Page 32, ibid; Page 37, Williamson's Marine Photo, Seattle; Page 40, lower photo, John Jobson; Page 42, top photo, *Fairbanks Daily News-Miner*; Page 44, Jimmy Bedford; Page 45, top-right photo, Russ Howlett; Page 46, lower-left photo, *Daily News-Miner*; Page 48, Jeff Phillips; Page 76, William W. Bacon III for *Daily News-Miner*.

About the Author

An ex-Associated Press correspondent and former managing editor of the *Fairbanks Daily News-Miner*, Kent Sturgis is a writer, photographer, editor and native-born Alaskan who has bounced back and forth between Seattle and the 49th state over the past 20 years. This is his first book. Sturgis is married to Pat Yockey and has three children—Tammy, Victoria and Christine.

And finally, thank you

Thanks to Lael Morgan for being a fine editor and great partner with high standards; to Dermot Cole and Mike Dalton for their good suggestions; to Chuck Gray for casting his practiced eye at the color reproduction; to Rocky MacDonald, for his boating skills at Russian Mission; and to all the Binkleys, especially Capt. Jim and Jim Jr., for their time and assistance that made this project possible.